CUTE KAWAII
DOODLES

CUTE KAWAII DOODLES

Over 100 super-cute doodles to draw

Sarah Alberto

ilex

An Hachette UK Company
www.hachette.co.uk

First published in Great Britain in 2018
by Ilex, a division of
Octopus Publishing Group Ltd
Carmelite House
50 Victoria Embankment
London EC4Y 0DZ
www.octopusbooks.co.uk

QUAR.KWAI

ISBN: 978-1-78157-633-5

A CIP catalogue record for this book is
available from the British Library.

Conceived, edited and designed by
Quarto Publishing plc, an imprint of
The Quarto Group
6 Blundell Street
London N7 9BH

Editor: Kate Burkett
Art editor: Martina Calvio
Designer: Karin Skånberg
Publisher: Samantha Warrington

Printed and bound in China
10 9 8 7 6 5 4 3 2 1

CONTENTS

MEET SARAH

Hi! My name is Sarah. I am a freelance illustrator and stay-at-home mum from Sydney, Australia. Art has always been a passion of mine, but it wasn't until 2015 that I started to take it more seriously and set up a YouTube channel under the pseudonym Doodles by Sarah.

As I became more active online, my love for arts and crafts grew. I was switching from planner to planner and trying out different kinds of scrapbooking, such as Project Life and mixed-media art. After that, I tried out art diaries and even exchanged snail mail with my fellow stationery enthusiasts.

It was when I started doodling on my planner that I received a lot of attention. I thought that it was more reasonable to just draw on my planner instead of buying stickers and stamps to decorate it, and my followers seemed to agree. So, I decided to stick with it and upload the content to my YouTube channel as 'doodle tutorials'. All my ideas for my videos are inspired by my children and my subscribers, who are always supporting my art and suggesting new things for me to draw.

My doodling journey has only just begun and I am excited to learn new things as I go, as well as collaborate with other people who are passionate about arts and crafts.

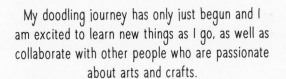

MATERIALS I USE

TOOLS FOR DOODLING

SARASA GEL PEN (BLACK)

For doodling my super-cute characters, my favourite tool to use is a ballpoint pen – in particular, a gel pen. Ballpoint pens are universal, affordable and versatile, and allow you to create small details and sharp lines. Just like fine liners, ballpoint pens come with different nibs – my favourites being 0.5, 0.7 and 0.38.

PENCIL

All of the doodles in this book are designed to be really simple, but if you are ever feeling unsure of your abilities, it's always best to start off your sketch with a pencil. Then, if you make a mistake, you can easily erase it and start again.

PAPER

I am a big fan of using gridded paper, as the lines serve as guides. However, feel free to use whatever kind of paper you like – there is plenty of blank space in this book for you to practise on.

TOOLS FOR COLOURING

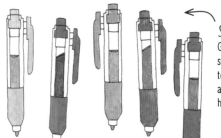

SARASA GEL PENS

Gel pens come in many different shades and colours. I use these to colour most of my drawings, as they give a really nice hand-drawn feel to my art.

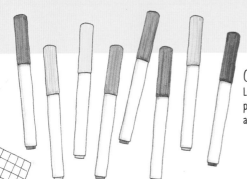

CRAYOLA SUPER TIPS WASHABLE MARKERS
Looking for affordable markers? These ones are perfect! They come in up to 50 different colours and they don't bleed through paper.

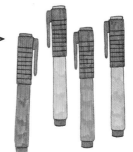

FABER–CASTEL PITT ARTIST PEN
Another favourite of mine! These brush pens are great for both colouring in and drawing.

SAKURA GELLY ROLL
I often use white gel pens to add more detail to some of my drawings.

TOMBOW DUAL BRUSH PENS
If you want to invest in good-quality markers for drawing or lettering, Tombow pens are perfect. In this book, I used the grey a lot for shadowing and detail work.

FACES AND PEOPLE

These different doodle expressions are made up of simple lines and shapes that are as easy as 1-2-3!

In this chapter, I will show you how I draw cute faces by combining dots and lines to create several looks. And let's not forget to add some hair!

BECAUSE I'M HAPPY

Changing features such as the eyebrows and mouth gives each face a different expression.

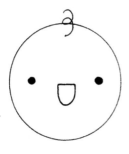

HAPPY DAYS!

Start with a basic smiley face, and then change each feature – eyebrows, eyes and mouth – in turn, coming up with as many variations as you can. You'll be amazed how much difference even one small alteration can make!

Yippeee!

FACES AND PEOPLE

HOW
ARE YOU
FEELING?

WHAT MOOD ARE YOU IN TODAY?

Bold or bashful? Down in the dumps or jumping for joy? How would you show each of these emotions?

EXPRESS YOURSELF

Drawing a shape similar to a smiling mouth above the eye gives your character a confused look.

EMOTIVE EMOJIS

Look at the emojis on your phone for some ideas, and then give
yourself half an hour and see how many different expressions
you can create. You'll probably find it's more than you expected!

Coloured lines added to the cheeks give this guy a sense of shame.

YOUR
GO!

THINK OUTSIDE THE BOX!

There are lots of instantly recognisable symbols that you can draw outside your character's face to show their moods and emotions. A question mark for confusion, an exclamation mark for surprise, a light bulb for those 'Eureka!' moments... How many more can you think of?

SMILEY FACE

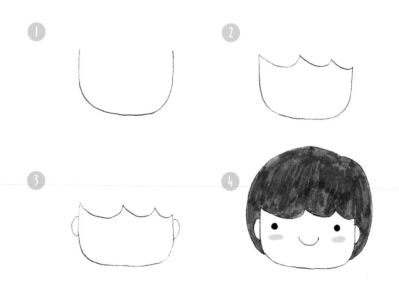

1

2

3

4

PULLING FACES

This guy doesn't look too pleased – he can't tame his curly mane!

MEAN AND MOODY

It's easy to make your character look happy, but what about when they're unhappy or grumpy? When someone frowns, for example, their eyebrows are drawn closer together; in a scowl the eyes are narrowed and the mouth turned down. See what a difference a small change can make.

NOT A HAIR OUT OF PLACE

Create a round shape for a sleek and smooth do.

He's not impressed with his fringe!

FRINGE BENEFITS!

Play around with different fringes – cut
straight across, wavy, spiky and so on.
As a general guideline, the hair takes up
roughly half the depth of the head – but
just have a go and see what looks right.

Draw a straight line across the forehead to alter the hairline.

COME UP WITH YOUR OWN COOL HAIRSTYLE!

BECOME A HAIRDRESSER

Long or short? Straight or curly? With or without a parting?
Practise drawing as many kinds of hair as you can.

FACE VALUE

NOT JUST A PRETTY FACE

THE EYES HAVE IT!

The eyes (open or closed) and eyebrows (straight or curved) are only a tiny
part of your character's face, but they speak volumes about his or her mood.

GOOD HAIR DAY

boohoo!

Add a circle to the top of her head to create a super-chic up-do!

CROWNING GLORIES!

Once you've decided on a hairstyle, jazz it up by adding colourful clips, bows, ribbons and scrunchies.

HOW DO YOU WEAR YOUR HAIR?

LOVELY LOCKS!

Sleek and smooth, frizzy and flyaway, neatly bobbed or flowing in long waves –
the hairstyle you choose will help convey your kawaii character's personality.

FOOD

Food is one of my favourite subjects to draw.
Who doesn't like food?

In this chapter, I will show you how to draw tasty
treats, such as pizza, popcorn and puddings, in six
easy steps or fewer!

Once you've got the basic shapes down, you can
add colour and cute faces to your doodles to give
them character and make them look even
more scrumptious!

BURRITO

UNDER WRAPS

Are you ga-ga for guacamole or a sucker for spice? Draw a burrito
with your favourite fillings. The shape of the wrap stays the same —
just change the colours and shapes inside.

BURRITO

LET THEM EAT CAKE

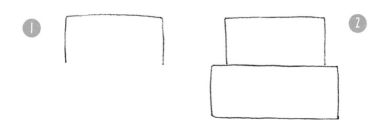

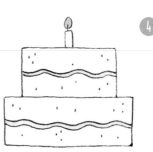

DIFFERENT DESSERTS

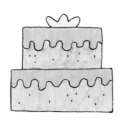

YUMMY

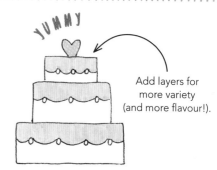

Add layers for more variety (and more flavour!).

GO DOOLALLY WITH YOUR DECORATIONS

Icing in almost every colour under the sun, from pastel pink
to zesty lime; cake pops in all kinds of shapes; multicoloured
sprinkles; sugar flowers; edible glitter – the sky's the limit.

CORN ON THE COB

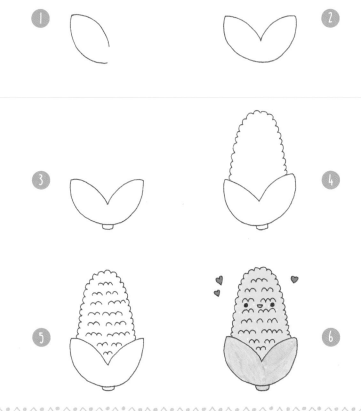

TRY IT FOR YOURSELF!

AMAZING MAIZE!

A few simple textural marks on the corn kernels and leaves really bring this doodle to life. You could adapt this doodle to make a knobbly artichoke – another super-easy way to get one of your five a day!

DELICIOUS DOUGHNUT

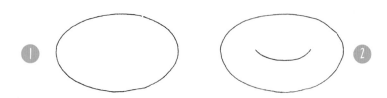

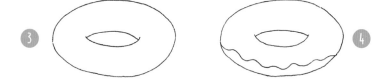

Add sprinkles to the doughnut to make it look even tastier!

ROUND AND ROUND WE GO...

We all know doughnuts are round – but they only look round when you view them from directly overhead. If you look at them from the side, as here, they're more of an oval shape. Be sure to draw the shapes you can actually see, not the shapes as you think they ought to be!

COFFEE HIT

○ ○

1

2

3

4

DRINK UP!

Add a straw to create a paper cup full of your favourite pop!

SLURP

Draw a clear container so you can see its contents.

○ ○

NOW DRAW IT!

Follow the steps opposite or try one of the options below for a different but equally delicious drink.

CHEERS!

Once you've got the hang of drawing a clear container, as in the variation opposite, you can doodle all kinds of drinks, from a classic cocktail complete with paper umbrella to a foaming pint of beer.

FRIES BEFORE GUYS

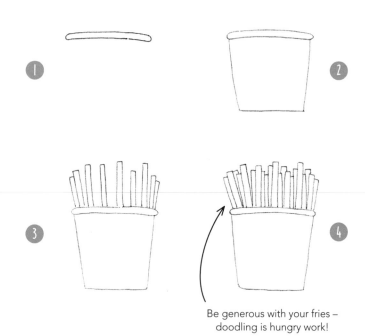

1 2 3

4

Be generous with your fries –
doodling is hungry work!

5

ALL BUNDLED UP!

You could use the same approach to draw a bunch of asparagus or coloured pencils in a pot or drinking straws in a beaker — just remember to make them different heights so they don't all merge together in a solid block.

NOW DRAW IT!

JUICY FRUITS

Add small circles for the strawberry's seeds.

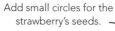

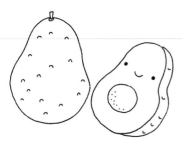

Drawing a face on your fruit creates that cute kawaii element!

COLOUR CO—ORDINATES

Draw the same doodle in different
sizes and citrussy colours to create a
whole array of tangy fruit — oranges,
lemons, limes and grapefruit.

DOODLE THE
INGREDIENTS OF
YOUR FAVOURITE
FRUIT SALAD!

TUTTI FRUTTI

Find as many different-coloured fruits as you can —
zingy green kiwi fruit, juicy red strawberries, tiny
purple blueberries — and create a kaleidoscope
of colour. Draw some fruits cut in half, as well
as whole ones, to make your doodles more interesting.

HAPPY HAMBURGER

 3

2

3

 4

5

 6

SUMMER SIZZLERS

Having a barbecue? This doodle would look great on an invitation
card! Add a smiley sun shining down from on high, a cooling drink
like the ones on page 42 and you're good to go.

HOT—DIGGITY—DOG

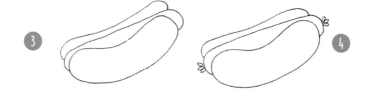

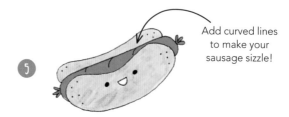

Add curved lines
to make your
sausage sizzle!

YOUR TURN!

SAUCE IT UP!

Don't forget the finishing touches! A squirt of
bright yellow mustard or red tomato ketchup
would spice this hot dog up a treat.

WE ALL SCREAM FOR ICE CREAM

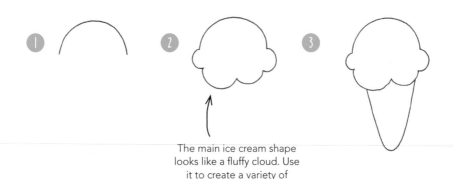

The main ice cream shape looks like a fluffy cloud. Use it to create a variety of ice-cream doodles!

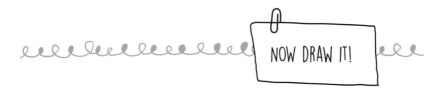
KNICKERBOCKER GLORY

Change the cone into a glass, fill it with layers of raspberry puree, ice cream and fresh fruit, and top with lashings of whipped cream. Then crown your super sundae with a wafer biscuit and a raspberry or two.

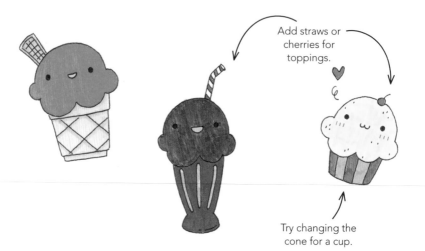

Add straws or cherries for toppings.

Try changing the cone for a cup.

DRAW YOUR OWN
DELICIOUS DESSERT!

SWEETS FOR MY SUGAR

What's your favourite dessert? Whether it's a tempting
trifle or a perfect pie, doodling lets you indulge your
sweet tooth without piling on the calories!

TASTY TOMATO

VERY CUTE VEGGIES

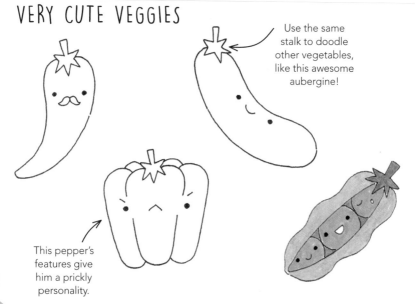

Use the same stalk to doodle other vegetables, like this awesome aubergine!

This pepper's features give him a prickly personality.

VEG OUT!

Zany carrots with green 'hair' tops, plump and friendly little spuds,
prim and proper sticks of celery all in a row: create a whole range
of veggie doodles, each with their own personality.

SALAD DAYS!

From crisp, round iceberg to tall and slender
romaine and spiky rocket, salad leaves come in
lots of luscious shades of green — so before you
chop them up for a healthy supper, why not turn
them into delicious doodles? Add a few perky
little radishes, resplendent in their red coats,
as a finishing touch.

DOODLE YOUR FAVOURITE SALAD!

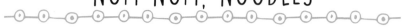

Simple shapes build up
to make the container
for your noodles.

1 ————

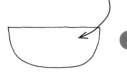 **2**

3

 **4**

5

 **6**

A TASTE OF THE ORIENT

For an authentic feel, decorate the bowls in a classic oriental colour combo, such as red and black or blue and white. Whatever colour or pattern you choose, be sure to fill your bowls with oodles of noodles! You can doodle strands of spaghetti in the same way.

GET TO
GRIPS WITH
NOODLES AND
CHOPSTICKS!

PRICKLY PINEAPPLE

Don't forget to add some dots for texture!

OPEN SESAME!

Why not have a go at doodling exotic fruit, such as pomegranates, star fruit or lychees? And don't just draw the outside — look for fruits that have pretty patterns or seeds inside when you cut them open.

PIZZA PARTY

Why not try out
different tasty
toppings?

PIZZA PIZZAZZ

You can't beat a good pizza! As the individual toppings in your pizza doodle will be very small, go for ingredients that are instantly recognisable by either their shape, such as slices of mushroom or pepperoni, or colour, such as black olives.

POPPING POPCORN

 1

 2

3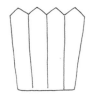

4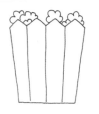

5

6

MOVIE MAGIC

Give your tub of popcorn a comfy seat so he can
enjoy his favourite movie — *Lord of the Fries,*
perhaps, or *Cakes on a Plane*?

ICE—COLD ICE LOLLY

1

2

3

4

FROZEN FRIENDS

Take a bite out of this lolly to give him brain freeze.

> TAKE A POP AT
> DOODLING YOUR
> FAVOURITE ICE LOLLY!

LOVELY LOLLIES

Chocolate-coated, fruit-flavoured, decorated or
plain – what's not to like? There are even lollies
shaped like rockets, balloons and stars... There
you go – the perfect excuse to do some 'research'!

SUPER SANDWICH

Add sneak peeks of your fillings to get mouths watering!

HAVE
A GO!

NICE SLICE!

Ring the changes by doodling different types of
bread. White with a lovely crust, granary speckled
with seeds, dark rye – try drawing different textures.

BREAD WINNERS

Give your sub a smiley face!

Add your favourite fillings!

PREPARE A
SANDWICH FOR
YOUR PACKED
LUNCH.

UPPER—CRUST SARNIES

Who says sandwiches have to be made from ready-sliced
bread? From baguettes to bagels, sub rolls to sourdoughs,
there's a whole world of bread to explore for delicious-looking
doodles! Can you get up to a baker's dozen?

TASTY TACO

Adding dots
to your filling
creates texture.

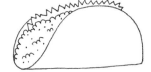

COOK UP A STORM!

Stuff your tacos full of flavoursome fillings –
chicken, beef, veggies and lots of hot chillies!

MILK IT

 1

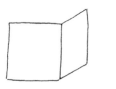 2

3

4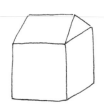

 5

 6

SLURP, SLURP!

Short and squat, tall and narrow — drink cartons come in many
different sizes. Think about how you can match the decoration
to the contents by playing with the colour of the label.

ANIMALS

Animals come in different shapes and sizes, colours and patterns. Here, I will share with you very easy steps on how to draw some of my favourites – from a normal house cat to the king of the jungle! And of course, I will be adding a sprinkle of kawaii to each and every one.

CATS

①

②

③

④

⑤

⑥

CUTE KITTENS

Use the same head shape to draw different kinds of cats, standing, sitting or sleeping.

NOW DRAW IT!

Have a go at drawing your purrfect puss on the blank space provided.

FELINE FROLICS

Follow the steps opposite or draw your very own feline friend. Start with easy 'poses' like the kittens opposite, and then move on to a cat or kitten playing.

KING OF THE JUNGLE

THE LION KING

This King of the Jungle looks a bit of a softy – a real pussycat! Create a whole pride of lions around him by leaving off the shaggy mane for the lionesses and drawing smaller doodles for the playful cubs.

BEAR HUG

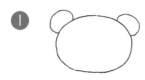

MANY BREEDS OF BEAR

Use different colours to create different breeds of bear.

BEAR NECESSITIES

A pointed snout, small ears and a rounded tummy will help make your
bear look cuddly and cute. Try out different colours, too – you don't
have to stick to what Mother Nature decrees!

BUNNY HOP

1

2

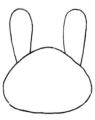

3

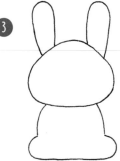

4

ALL EARS

Play around with the bunny's ears – draw them standing up to show your character is alert, or droopy to give it that cute and floppy look.

FUNNY BUNNIES

How many different expressions can you give your bunnies? Happy, sad,
relaxed, frightened: it's all in the tilt of the ears and the shape of the mouth.

A DOG'S LIFE

A DIFFERENT BREED

Draw different breeds of dogs by changing the shape of the ears, nose and mouth.

MAN'S BEST FRIEND!

Try doodling a dog bounding along after a ball or even sitting up and begging for a bone. You'd have to be barking mad not to give it a go!

AN ELEPHANT NEVER FORGETS

1

2

3

4

Add some lines to the trunk to give your elephant its wrinkly skin.

5

6

JOYFUL JUMBOS

Doodle a whole family of elephants in a row, each holding on to the tail of the one in front with its trunk. Start with the big bull at the front and work your way down to a tiny calf at the back – and give them nice, happy smiles!

FISHING FOR COMPLIMENTS

NOW DRAW IT!

There are plenty of fish in the sea. Draw your favourites here!

SOMETHING FISHY GOING ON?

Create a whole shoal of fantastic fish! Vary the shape of the tail and fins and go wild with your colours and patterns.

GRACEFUL GIRAFFE

SPOT THE DIFFERENCE!

They say a leopard can't change its spots, but there's no reason why your giraffe
shouldn't! How many fantabulous colour combos can you come up with?

MOTHER HEN

1

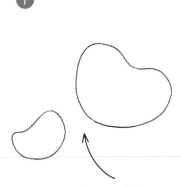

Draw a jellybean shape for the bodies of both mother and chick!

2

3

4

CLUCKETY, CLUCK!

Add a clutch of eggs, and maybe even a chick hatching
out of its shell, to your poultry picture so that your
mother hen has something to cluck about.

MOTHER HEN

CHEEKY MONKEY

1

2

3

4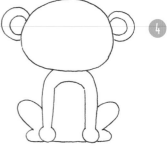

5

6

ANIMALS

MONKEY BUSINESS

Why not draw your monkey swinging from the branch of a tree by his tail
or eating a banana? Don't forget to give him a cheeky grin!

QUIET AS A MOUSE

1

2

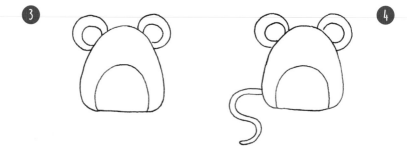

3

4

5

6

A MISCHIEF OF MICE

Did you know that the collective name for a group of mice is a mischief of mice? How mischievous can you make your mice look?

PLUMP PENGUIN

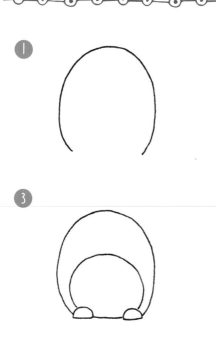

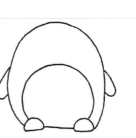

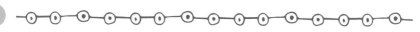

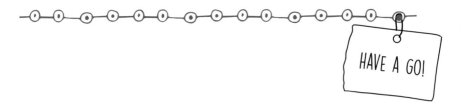

PENGUINS AT PLAY

Penguins look quite comical shuffling along on land – but
if you give your little penguins a big white iceberg to slide
down into the sea, they'll be in their element!

PORKY PIG

ANIMALS

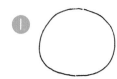

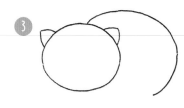

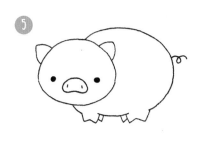

OINK, OINK!

This little piggy went to market, this little piggy
stayed at home... Where will your little piggies go?

A WHALE OF A TIME

FRIENDLY FACES

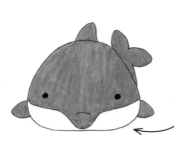

Change the face of your sea creature to create an orca or a dolphin!

THERE SHE BLOWS!

Draw your whale spouting water as she surfaces from beneath the waves.

FANTASY

The key to drawing unique characters and objects is
to use your imagination. In this chapter, I will show
you how to draw simple, make-believe characters,
such as a unicorn, a genie, a mermaid and a wizard.
Feel free to personalise your doodles – why not give
your witch a wand to cast her spells?

THE MAGIC DRAGON

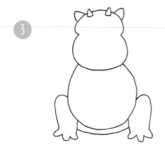

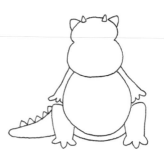

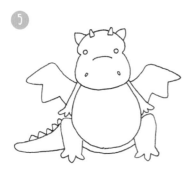

FIRE YOUR IMAGINATION

When they're not breathing flames through their nostrils and scorching innocent passers-by, dragons are traditionally found guarding hoards of golden treasure. What can you draw for your dragon to protect?

THE MAGIC DRAGON

YOUR FAIRY GODMOTHER

Give your fairy spell-casting abilities by adding in a wand complete with stars and sparkles.

A SPRINKLING OF STARDUST

Your fairy godmother needs plenty of magic stardust to make all those wishes come true. Draw her wand with multicoloured trails of light and sparkling stars shooting out of it. Cinderella, you *shall* go to the ball!

GENIE IN A BOTTLE

Fold the genie's arms to give him the authority he needs to grant all those wishes.

PURE GENIE—US!

Pair your genie with the magic lamp on
page 122 for a magical extravaganza straight
out of *One Thousand and One Nights*.

GHOST TOWN

FRIEND OR FOE?

Play around with your ghosts'
expressions and see how many
different characters you can come up
with. Will you draw your ghosts with a
sweet smile or a gruesome grin?

HAUNTED HOUSE

1

2

3

4

5

6

DRAW MORE
HAIR-RAISING HOUSES HERE!

HOUSE OF HORRORS

Tumbledown turrets, a gravestone or three in the garden, bats silhouetted against a full moon: the more horrifying you can make your haunted house, the better. No self-respecting ghoul would settle for a neat little semi-detached!

ALADDIN'S LAMP

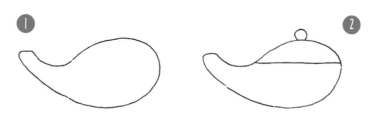

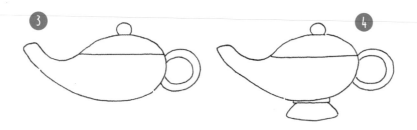

Add designs to your lamp to make it more interesting and specific to your genie.

△ ● ▽ ● △ ● ▽ ● △ ● ▽ ● △ ● ▽ ● △ ● ▽ ● △ ● ▽

```
                                              ○
                                            NOW
                                         DRAW IT!
```

ABRACADABRA!

Add plenty of sparks and stars shooting
out of the spout of your lamp to give it
that all-important magical feel.

▽ ● △ ● ▽ ● △ ● ▽ ● △ ● ▽ ● △ ● ▽ ● △ ● ▽ ● △ ● ▽ ● △

THE LITTLE MERMAID

TRY IT
YOURSELF!

MAKE A SPLASH
Give your mermaid some friends
to play with by changing the
hairstyles and tail colours.

MONSTER MASH

CREATE YOUR VERY OWN CREEPY CREATURES!

MIX AND MIS—MATCH

How many different features can you combine to make your monster? If you matched, say, the shaggy mane of one creature with the tusks of another and the big googly eyes of a third, you'd end up with something quite outrageous!

YIKES!

A PIRATE'S LIFE FOR ME

AHOY, ME HEARTIES!

Once you've drawn your pirate, give him some accessories — perhaps a patch over one eye, or a wooden leg, or a sabre to swipe at his enemies. And don't forget his treasure chest, full of golden trinkets and pieces of eight!

BLAST OFF!

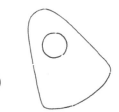
1

2

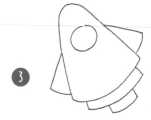
3

4

TAKE FLIGHT

Plumes of smoke show that this rocket's engine is running to full capacity.

ROCKET PEOPLE

Draw an astronaut to pilot your rocket. Maybe he or she
could be doing a space walk or looking down at the Earth
far below while comets and asteroids hurtle past.

OUT OF THIS WORLD

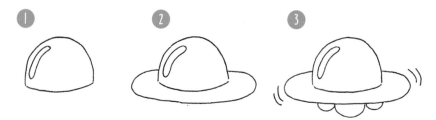

SUPER SPACESHIPS

Different shapes create different bodies for your UFOs.

SPACE ODDITIES

Alien spacecraft come in lots of shapes – flying saucers, vessels that look like giant cigars and even black triangle shapes. What kind of craft might the creepy creatures you created on page 126 devise for themselves?

OTHERWORLDLY UNICORN

PERSONALISE YOUR
UNICORN BY GIVING
IT DIFFERENT—
COLOURED HAIR

MAKE YOUR UNICORN UNIQUE!

In legend, unicorns are often said to be pure white, but
as few, if any, people have actually seen one, you can
make yours any colour under the sun, or even rainbow-
coloured. These magical creatures deserve nothing less!

VAMPIRE

1

2

3

4

5

6

VAMP UP YOUR VAMPIRE!

My Dracula is super cool, with a slicked-back hairstyle and flowing black cape. Maybe yours could look a bit more wild and wicked? A few drops of blood dripping from those vicious fangs should do the trick...

VAMPIRE

WICKED WITCH

1

2

3

4

5

6

TOOLS OF THE TRADE

What else does your witch need? As well as a broomstick, every wicked witch should have a cauldron to brew up her evil potions and a crystal ball to see into the future, not to mention a black cat to give her a helping hand (or paw).

WIZENED WIZARD

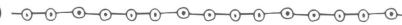

1

2

3

4

5

6

WIZARD ATTIRE

Choose rich, deep colours for your wizard's robes and
pointy hat (purple, royal blue, red, gold and silver are
popular choices in the wizarding world) and decorate them
with magical symbols such as moons and stars.

SEASONS AND HOLIDAYS

Winter, spring, summer and autumn.
With the seasons come different holidays.
In this chapter, I will show you how to draw simple
items that represent the seasons and some of
the traditions and festivities that go along with
each holiday.

AUTUMN LEAVES

FABULOUS FOLIAGE

What captures the feeling of autumn better than an array of falling leaves? Use rich, warm colours in every imaginable shade, from sunshine yellow and gold through to rich reds and russets.

BEACH BALL

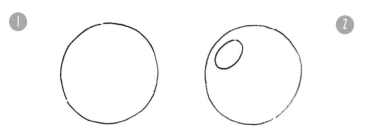

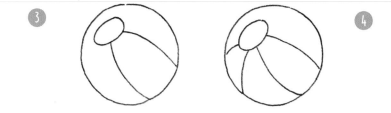

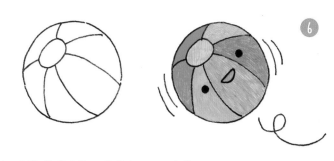

BOUNCING BALL

A beach ball is a must-have on a summer beach holiday. Angle the ball
slightly sideways and add a few curved lines on either side to make it
look as if it's bouncing. See how the segments are wider at the back
than at the front? If you drew them all the same size, your doodle
would just look like a flat circle rather than a round ball.

BURNING BONFIRE

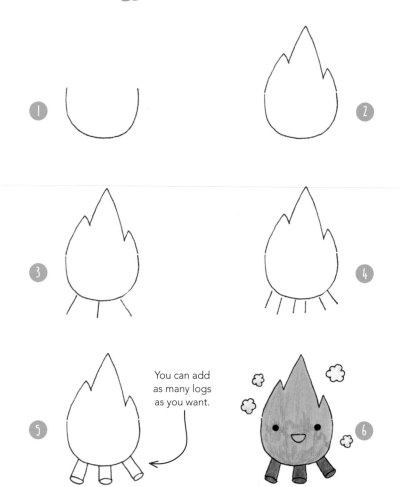

You can add
as many logs
as you want.

YOUR TURN!

REMEMBER, REMEMBER, THE 5TH OF NOVEMBER...

You can't have Bonfire Night without a bonfire! Add some rockets, Catherine wheels, Roman candles and other fireworks to make the occasion go with a bang.

BUTTERFLIES (AND BEES) IN YOUR STOMACH

Decorate your butterfly's wings with any pattern you wish.

USE THE BUTTERFLY'S BODY TO CREATE A BUZZING BEE!

FLIGHT OF THE BUMBLEBEE
To make it look as if your bumblebee is in flight, add a looping, broken line that shows where it's just been.

FLOWERS IN BLOOM

SPRING IS IN THE AIR!

The first flowers in the garden are a sure sign that spring has sprung! To celebrate, doodle a whole array of blooms, from pots of daffs and daisies to floating water lilies — or even invent your very own floral fantasies.

CREATE A BOUQUET TO GIVE TO YOUR BESTIE!

BLOOMIN' LOVELY!

I've given you lots of ideas for different-shaped flower heads and petals, but try and come up with a few of your own. What about trumpet shapes for lilies and daffodils, or overlapping heart-shaped petals for a beautiful rosebud?

TRICK OR TREAT

PUMPKIN HEADS

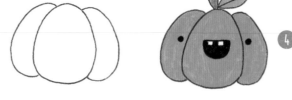

SKETCH A SPOOKY
TREAT!

HALLOWEEN LANTERNS

Doodle spooky pumpkin lanterns in different sizes and colours,
all in a row, to decorate an invitation to a Halloween party.

A (SAND)CASTLE FIT FOR A KING

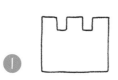
1

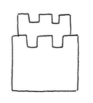
2

3

4

SUPER SANDCASTLES

Adding some dots will give the sand texture.

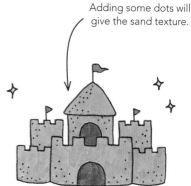

SEASONS AND HOLIDAYS

FANCY FORTIFICATIONS

Give your sandcastle windows and doors made of shells, top the turrets
with flags and add a moat to keep out intruders!

SEASHELLS

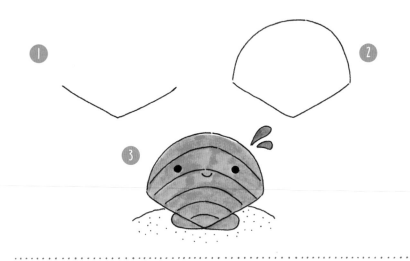

A TRIO OF SHELLS

SHELL SHAPES

The cockle and scallop-type shells I've doodled are only two possible shapes
out of many. Why not try drawing a nautilus shell curving round in a gracious
spiral, a purple-blue mussel or a cone-shaped limpet with spiky ridges?

FROSTY THE SNOWMAN

1

2

3

4

5

6

WINTER WARMERS

As well as a scarf in your favourite football team's colours, give your
snowman or snow-woman earmuffs and a snuggly hat to keep out the cold.

STARFISH

○ ○

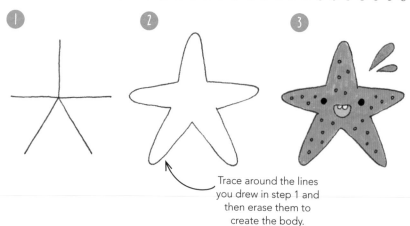

Trace around the lines you drew in step 1 and then erase them to create the body.

A GALAXY OF STARFISH

Play around with the shape and texture of each starfish. They can be bumpy, long, thin or curvy.

○ ○

TEST YOUR
STARFISH SKILLS!

SUPER STAR

Keep the lines around the outside of the starfish shape loose and fluid, or even a bit wobbly — it's a living creature, after all, and you don't want it to look too rigid. Its 'arms' can even be slightly different lengths.

CHRISTMAS STOCKINGS

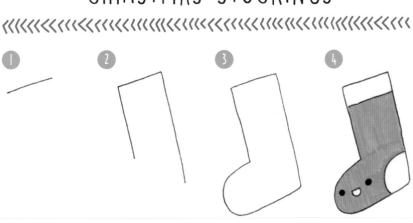

··

HANG YOUR STOCKINGS BY THE FIRE

Don't just stick to one size. You can draw your stockings short, long or extra long!

〈〈

CREATE AND COLOUR!

Red, green and gold are the obvious choices for Christmassy colours and
always look good together, but feel free to experiment. Go on – set all
your coloured pens out on the table and have fun playing around!

YOUR TURN!

LIVING OUT OF A SUITCASE

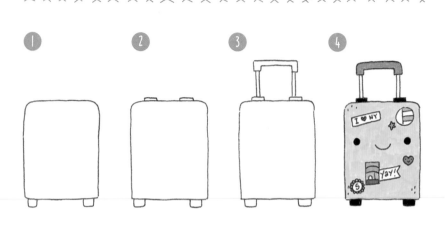

1 2 3 4

OFF WE GO!

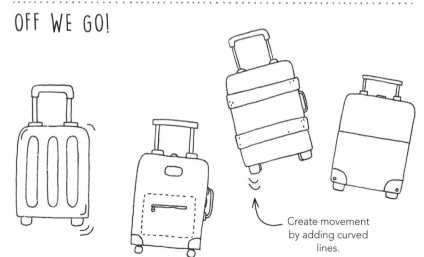

Create movement
by adding curved
lines.

PACK YOUR BAGS!

Have fun giving your bags and cases different characters. For example, while a hard-shell case like the ones shown opposite looks like a bit of a tough nut, a Gladstone bag has more olde-worlde charm and a briefcase would be suitably brisk and businesslike.

THROW SHADE TO THE SUN

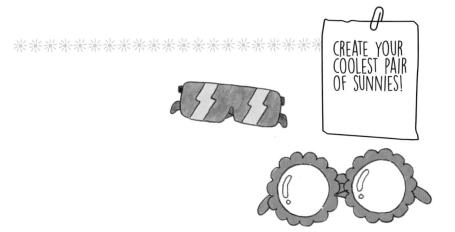

CREATE YOUR COOLEST PAIR OF SUNNIES!

COOL AS A CUCUMBER

From diamante-encrusted frames to wacky designs shaped like birds' wings, the right pair of sunnies will keep your kawaii characters looking super cool.

SURF'S UP!

① ② ③

A BOARD FOR EVERY OCCASION

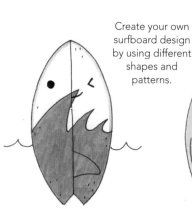

Create your own surfboard design by using different shapes and patterns.

KYLE

Or why not personalise it by adding your name?

YO, DUDE!

Surfboards are as colourful as the characters who ride them. They come in different shapes, too: some are long and pointed at both ends; some are more stumpy and rounded; some have a swallowtail-shaped fin. Be creative and give your board a personality all of its own.

ITSY-BITSY BIKINI

 1

 2

 3

 4

5

HERE COMES THE SUN!

Whether it has two straps, a halter neck or is strapless, have your
characters cool off in a snazzy bikini. You can draw the same fabric
for top and bottom, or make one section plain and the other patterned –
just make sure the colours go together.

Go for polka dots, stars or stripes to make your bathing costume stand out!

CHIC SWIMSUIT

Have a go at designing a one-piece. There's much more fabric to doodle
on — try adding spots, stripes or different prints for a playful yet stylish look.

WATERING CAN

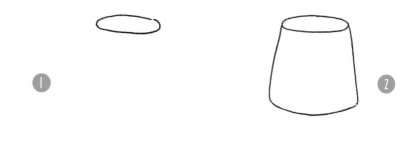

HOW DOES YOUR GARDEN GROW?

With a bit of help from your friendly watering can, of course! You could also doodle
a zany garden hose, running around in circles to give all the plants a thirst-quenching drink.

OH, CHRISTMAS TREE!

TWINKLE, TWINKLE

Add decorations for a truly festive feeling!

NOW DRAW IT!

DECORATIVE DELIGHTS

Try doodling red-and-white striped candy canes, giant snowflakes,
brightly coloured baubles and strings of fairy lights – make your
Christmas tree as eye-catching as you can!

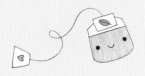

DAILY LIFE

Some of my favourite things to doodle are the items
lying around at home. Sketching furniture, cutlery
or even the things inside your bag is a great way
of practising. In this chapter, I will share quick and
easy steps on how to doodle random
everyday objects.

TAKE FLIGHT

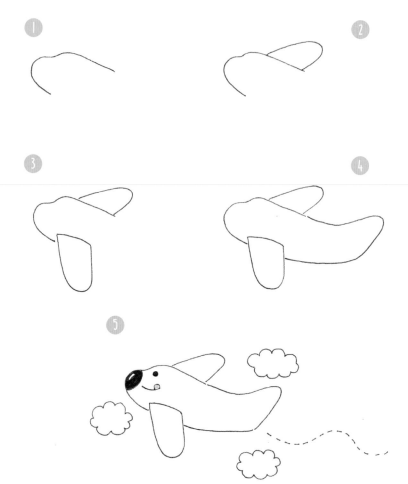

'COPTER CAPERS

By changing the shape a bit and adding a set of whirring rotor blades,
you can turn your plane into a plucky little search-and-rescue helicopter.

BAG OF TRICKS

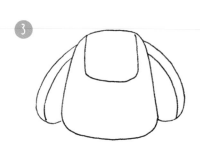

△ ● ▽ ● △ ● ▽ ● △ ● ▽ ● △ ● ▽ ● △ ● ▽ ● △ ● ▽ ● △ ● ▽

BACK TO BASICS

Try adding different colours and patterns to your backpack.
Alternatively, you could make it bigger and add a sturdy
metal frame to turn it into a rucksack for hiking.

▽ ● △ ● ▽ ● △ ● ▽ ● △ ● ▽ ● △ ● ▽ ● △ ● ▽ ● △ ● ▽ ● △

△ • ▽ • △ • ▽ • △ • ▽ • △ • ▽ • △ • ▽ • △ • ▽ • △ • ▽ • △ • ▽

▽ • △ • ▽ • △ • ▽ • △ • ▽ • △ • ▽ • △ • ▽ • △ • ▽ • △ • ▽ • △ • ▽ • △

△ • ▽ △ • ▽ • △ • ▽ • △ • ▽ • △ • ▽ • △ • ▽ • △ • ▽

NOW
DRAW
IT!

WHAT'S IN YOUR BAG?

Does your backpack contain make-up or notes and
pens for doodling? Sketch the contents of your bag.

▽ • △ • ▽ • △ • ▽ • △ • ▽ • △ • ▽ • △ • ▽ • △ • ▽ • △

AND SO TO BED...

1

2

3

4

5

6

YOUR TURN!

ZZZZZZ!

Soft furnishings make lovely doodles, too! A plump pillow, eyes tightly closed, might be dreaming up all kinds of adventures.

A CLEAN SWEEP

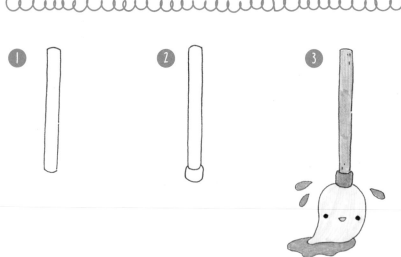

CAN YOU HANDLE IT?

What other long-handled household tools could you draw?
How about a garden spade or a hoe? Or an extendible
duster? While you're at it, don't forget about all the
things that go with these items — like a bucket for
the mop, a dustpan for the broom and a wheelbarrow
for the garden tools.

A CLEAN SWEEP

CACTUS

▽ △ ▽ △ ▽ △ ▽ △ ▽ △ ▽ △ ▽ △ ▽ △ ▽ △ ▽ △ ▽ △ ▽ △ ▽ △ ▽ △ ▽

Simple shapes build up to make the cactus.

▽ △ ▽ △ ▽ △ ▽ △ ▽ △ ▽ △ ▽ △ ▽ △ ▽ △ ▽ △ ▽ △ ▽ △ ▽ △ ▽ △ ▽

▽ △ ▽ △ ▽ △ ▽ △ ▽ △ ▽ △ ▽ △ ▽ △ ▽ △ ▽ △ ▽ △ ▽

HAVE A GO!

SIMPLE SUCCULENTS

Try drawing other types of cacti, such as a prickly pear,
which has flattened 'pads', or the saguaro, which has
'branches' coming off a main trunk. You can create
the prickly spines with just a few dashes of your pen.

CACTUS

▽ △ ▽ △ ▽ △ ▽ △ ▽ △ ▽ △ ▽ △ ▽ △ ▽ △ ▽ △ ▽ △ ▽

GREEN FINGERS

POTTED PLANTS

Try doodling pots of ferns, flowers and succulents. The more colourful, the better!

Create different plant pots by
drawing shapes such as hexagons,
squares and cylinders.

GO POTTY!

You can grow plants in all sorts of weird and wonderful
containers, from old milk churns and wheelbarrows to
wellington boots. Have a look around your home and see
what unusual 'pots' you could draw your plants in.

PICTURE PERFECT

XXXXXX XXXXXXXXXXXXXXXX X X X X

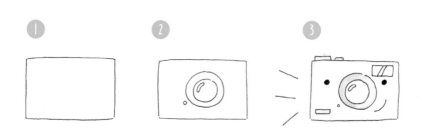

CLICK, CLICK, FLASH

A camera has three basic parts – a lens, flash and buttons!

XXXXXXXXXXXXXXXXXXXXX X X X X

SAY 'CHEESE'!

What has your camera captured? Doodles of photos are a good way of showing what's happening 'offstage', outside the main action of your picture.

MUSIC TO MY EARS

1

2

3

4

5

6

ACCESSORISE YOUR KAWAII CREATIONS

A simple object, like these headphones or a book or guitar, can speak volumes. What objects would you select to give an insight into your kawaii character's interests?

A RAY OF LIGHT

LET THERE BE LIGHT!

A few simple pen strokes are all you need to
convey rays of light shining from a bulb.

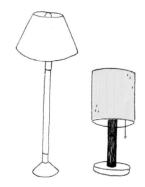

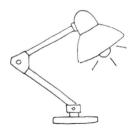

DESIGN YOUR OWN LAMP!

SWITCH IT UP

Have a go at doodling desk lamps and floor lamps with different shades.

A RAY OF LIGHT

LUSCIOUS LIPS

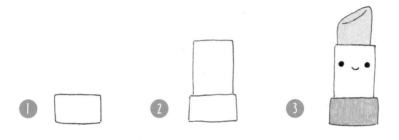

SEALED WITH A KISS

Don't neglect the packaging – this polka-dot lid is stylish and it protects your lippy.

COLOUR ME BEAUTIFUL

What kind of personality do different lipstick colours convey?
Berry red for a vamp, pretty pink for a party princess, black
for a goth... These are just a few possibilities.

KISS AND MAKE-UP

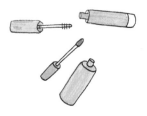

TEXTURE TRICKS

As well as the shapes and colours, think about the texture of the
things you're doodling. A few small dots will suggest the softness
of a powder puff, and a couple of lines will indicate the reflective
surface of a mirror: it's all in the detail!

Practise by drawing the cosmetics you use in the bathroom.

BATHROOM BEAUTIES

Bubble bath in shades of blue and green, jars of face
cream, even humble toothpaste tubes – who'd have
thought your bathroom cupboard held so much potential?

CALL ME!

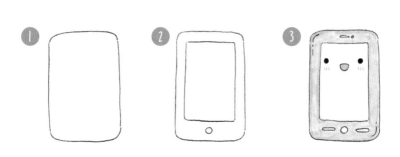

HOLD THE PHONE

Most phones are touch screen now, but you can still draw a keypad to add more variety.

BRRRRING, BRRRRING!

How might you show that the phone is ringing? Maybe you could add a loudspeaker symbol or musical notes alongside it?

CUP OF COFFEE

1

2

3

FULL TO THE BRIM

Change the shape
of the container by
creating different line
strokes. Make your
lines curvy, straight or
slanted.

WAKE UP AND SMELL THE COFFEE!

Kill two birds with one stone — make yourself an early-morning cuppa, and then use it to get in some doodling practice!

PRETTY AND POLISHED

① ② ③

BOTTLE IT UP

Mix and match the top and bottom of your bottles to create new shapes!

YOU'VE NAILED IT!

Raid your make-up bag and draw any bottles of nail
varnish you find inside. Don't forget to add small white
lines to the glass bottles and any metallic elements
to show that they're reflective and catch the light.

PLAYING WITH COLOUR

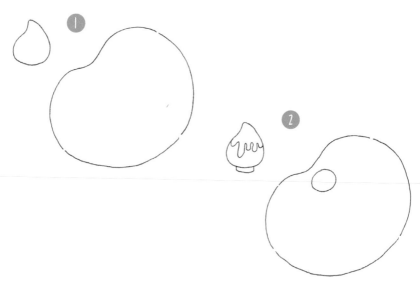

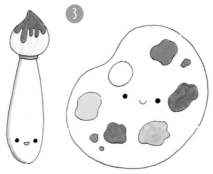

ARTISTIC LICENCE

A kidney-shaped palette is a must for any artist. Cover yours in colourful
splashes and splodges – the range of colours is entirely up to you!

TUNE IN

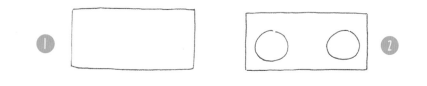

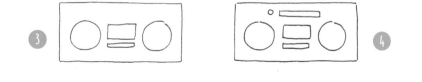

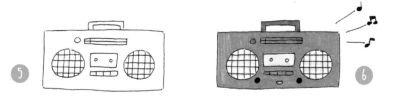

HAVE A GO!

MUSIC, MAESTRO!
If you're a music lover, a really old-fashioned record player, complete
with trumpet-shaped speaker, would make a lovely doodle.

TABLE TALK

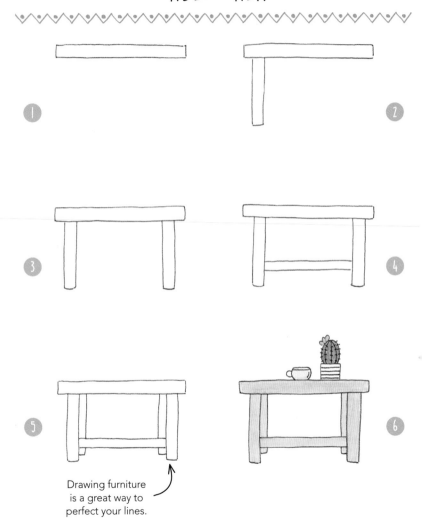

1

2

3

4

5

6

Drawing furniture
is a great way to
perfect your lines.

A BIT OF A POLISH!

Many pieces of furniture can be drawn with just a few straight
lines, so this is a great way to polish up your doodling skills.
Give it a go whenever you've got a few minutes to spare.

TEA PARTY

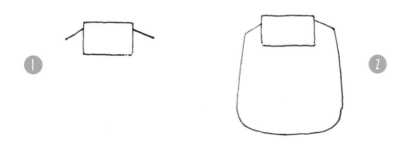

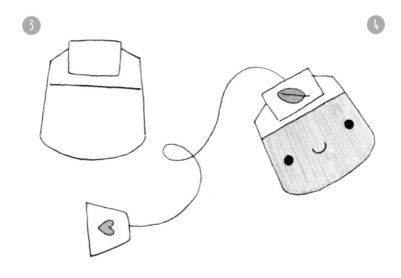

WHAT'S YOUR FAVOURITE HERBAL TEA?

TEA FOR TWO...

Draw the china for a tea party and give each piece – cup and saucer, teapot, milk jug and bowl full of sugar cubes – its own expression.

TOOLS OF THE TRADE

DIY DOODLES

Dust off those old hammers and chisels and use them as your inspiration for a whole series of handy characters – you're sure to hit the nail on the head!

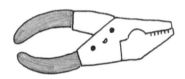

FRIENDLY FACES

Give your tools friendly faces. Hopefully they'll
encourage a day of DIY about the house!

WASHER DRYER

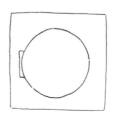

ALL IN A SPIN!

Laundry day needn't be a total washout! While you're waiting for your smalls to stop spinning, use the time to doodle your washer dryer and other household appliances. For a vintage feel, you could even go back in time and draw an old hand-cranked mangle!

NOW DRAW IT!

WHATEVER THE WEATHER

COME RAIN OR SHINE...

Smiley suns, clouds sprinkling rain or being blown across the sky, streaks of lightning, colourful rainbows... Look at the symbols on weather maps to get some ideas for your meteorological doodles.

FORECAST

What is the weather
like where you
are today?

PULL YOUR WEIGHT

①  ②

③  ④

⑤ 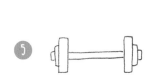  ⑥

TRY IT YOURSELF!

WEIGHTY MATTERS

Take time out from being a gym bunny and draw some exercise equipment — it's a lot easier than actually working out! Dumb-bells, medicine balls and kettlebells are all easy shapes to start with.

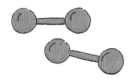

FOR MY
PARENTS